HAPPY VALLEY SCHOOL

A History and Remembrance

Tom Riley

HERITAGE BOOKS
2015

HERITAGE BOOKS
AN IMPRINT OF HERITAGE BOOKS, INC.

Books, CDs, and more—Worldwide

For our listing of thousands of titles see our website
at
www.HeritageBooks.com

Published 2015 by
HERITAGE BOOKS, INC.
Publishing Division
5810 Ruatan Street
Berwyn Heights, Md. 20740

Copyright © 2015 Tom Riley

Heritage Books by the author:

Happy Valley School: A History and Remembrance

Orphan Train Riders: A Brief History of the Orphan Trail Era (1854–1929) with Entrance Records from the American Female Guardian Society's Home for the Friendless in New York Volume One

Orphan Train Riders: Entrance Records from the American Female Guardian Society's Home for the Friendless in New York Volume Two

The Orphan Train to Destiny

All rights reserved. No part of this book may be reproduced or transmitted in any form or by any means, electronic or mechanical, including photocopying, recording or by any information storage and retrieval system without written permission from the author, except for the inclusion of brief quotations in a review.

International Standard Book Numbers
Paperbound: 978-0-7884-3170-8
Clothbound: 978-0-7884-6189-7

DEDICATION

This book is dedicated to all the children who grew up at Happy Valley School and who went on to become good citizens of the American Dream. Many of those children grew up and served ably in the cause of freedom everywhere and are pillars of their community. It is also dedicated to my wife, Cruey, who taught me the real meaning of family, and to my daughters, Professor Gina Riley-Daly and Dr. Bernadette Riley, and to Benjamin Noah Riley, my grandson.

FOREWORD

In writing *Happy Valley School: A History and Remembrance* I make no claim to writing the definitive book on that institution. This book is the result of my interest in exploring the growth of a unique institution, The Five Points House of Industry, from its early inception as a private charitable foundation in 1850 to its location in Pomona, New York, in 1911 under the name of Happy Valley Colony. Any mistakes or omissions are solely the responsibility of the author. I wanted to share with my fellow alumni some of the research I had uncovered. And, as President of the Rockland County Genealogical Society, I hope it aids future historians and genealogists.

I want to thank the following people for their help in supplying me with material and old photographs that I hope makes this book interesting. I was heartened when an eighty-one- year-old, former Happy Valley alumna called me from Florida to tell me I had uncovered a picture of her father when he came to visit her. The family was from Greece. Claude Boorum, Jr., son of the first superintendent of Happy Valley Colony, deserves special credit for filling me in on the early development of Happy Valley. This wonderful man, then eighty-three, shared with me many Kodak Brownie photographs his father had taken years ago. He was born and raised on the grounds of Happy Valley until he left with his family in 1930.

I would like to thank John Kearns, a special friend, now deceased, and his family for their help in supplying me with photographs. His long tenure as recreation director and his interest in recording the times makes this an informative book. I would also like to thank Fort Wilkerson for his kindness; he worked as a social worker in the mid 60's and he passed along some interesting books, one dating back to 1851. It was a novella and it was written by women to raise funds for the building of the Five Points House of Industry.

I want to thank the staff of the Historical Society of Rockland County, especially Myra and Melanie Solomen for letting me help them organize records and material from Greer Woodycrest which was stored away uncatalogued in an old barn until I showed an interest in researching material relating to HV (Happy Valley). They promptly put me to work and I found some information relating to Happy Valley School and a treasure trove of Americana relating to the Orphan Train Era. I would like to thank the late Peter Krell of the historical society who gave me an Annual Report for 1969 which spurred me on to further research. I would also like to thank the family of the late Albie Mills for sharing recollections of the early years he spent at HV with his father, the legendary Mr. Mills, our shop teacher.

I would like to thank Tim Henderson of the *Rockland Journal News* for allowing me to reprint an article he wrote on a Happy Valley reunion organized by Haya Khoury, Jim Ashcroft, Pete Carney and others. Mr. George Ashforth, a Yale graduate and Executive Director of Happy Valley School for a long time, is eighty-four years old and living in Connecticut. He sent his best wishes to the Alumni Association in a phone call. Mr. Walter Hendricksen passed away a number of years ago but his wife Adne and their children remain in our thoughts. And to all the housemothers and housefathers who ably served us, we say *thank you*.

HAPPY VALLEY SCHOOL: A HISTORY AND REMEMBRANCE

On Sunday, July 19, 1992 a very special gathering took place. People from many states and the greater New York area drove on to the grounds of the Crystal Run School in Pomona, New York, for an alumni gathering that was the culmination of a labor of nostalgia and love for the Happy Valley of our youth. Haya Khoury, a New York City Corporation Council lawyer and a Happy Valley alumnus, had arranged the affair, with the help of countless others, so that a fitting goodbye could be said to a special place in time, the Happy Valley of our youth. Crystal Run School had been Happy Valley School from 1911 to 1973. In three months workers would be turning it into a golf course.

As each car rode onto the grounds, cries of recognition would go up and embraces and jokes revived long ago memories of the way we were. The transformation from homeless and neglected children had been complete. Now bankers, carpenters, designers, teachers, laborers, photographers, builders, postal workers and a lawyer talked animatedly about the days they shared as children. They gazed into each other's eyes searchingly for the child they remembered.

Some had stood up well to the years while others showed on their faces the struggle it took to be where they were today. All accepted each other with spontaneity and generosity. The Ashcrofts Carneys, Khourys, Greys, Grippers, Rileys, Reineckes, Wenzs and Towles and many other alumni families found warmth, nostalgia, and joy in the company of each other.

I remember the day I arrived at Happy Valley as if it were yesterday. Feelings bring recall easily to mind. The car drove slowly unto the grounds as acres of green fields and apple trees slipped by. As we passed by a huge building we looked at the faces of kids who stared back at us with the same wonder and absorption only kids possess. My brothers and my sister and I took it all in with anxiety and pangs of homesickness from being uprooted from a nine month stay with foster parents. This was going to be different and little did I know that I would grow to love Happy Valley. For ten years it was home to me.

Happy Valley was truly integrated. Black, White, Hispanic, Jew and Arabic slept side by side, ate, played and worked together. The common denominator was family dysfunction; neglect, abuse and poverty had brought them all together. Although we had house-parents around, the warmth, camaraderie and interaction was with one's peers. You fought, made friends and felt the first pangs of adolescent love with your peers. The mystery of life was very real and so much was unknown only to be revealed as maturity unfolded.

We had 311 acres to roam in. Wildlife, nature and domesticated animals were all around us. We built tree houses, underground forts and made our own bows and arrows. We hunted snapping turtles in the wetlands and caught frogs and salamanders in streams. We overturned old boards and rocks looking for snakes. We grew some of our own food and had fresh milk daily from cows kids milked. We learned so many sports and games from Coach Kearns. We learned how to win, how to take a loss, fight fair and be a good sport. We marked the seasons by the games we played. We had no cars so running and biking was second nature. Happy Valley was known for its runners and athletes. Sanchez and Blanchett received accolades in Cross Country and Jimmy Ashcroft became a world-class runner and Rockland County Hall of Famer in the 100 meters. The love of athletics imbued character into so many boys and girls at Happy Valley School.

And when we came of age and discovered girls a whole new world revealed itself. Anxiety and shyness had to be overcome only with time. Acne, hairstyles and clothes became major concerns and learning how to dance was fraught with embarrassment. The post-game dances were as important as the game itself.

That's what I remember about Happy Valley. We all still had a lot of growing and learning to do, but it gave a bunch of kids a good foundation on which to build their lives. The topography of Happy Valley may change but one had the feeling Happy Valley was more of a place in time and of the heart. Judging by the number of people who turned up that summer day, Happy Valley will be remembered, for sure.

On my last visit to the grounds where Happy Valley once stood I felt I must write a history and remembrance of that place in time, the Happy Valley of our youth. As bulldozers turned cottages I once lived in to rubble, the familiar landmarks of memory were being torn asunder and there was a danger that a place that had been home to thousands of impoverished children might be forgotten. Haya Khoury and many other alumni felt there was something special about Happy Valley School that was worth remembering and celebrating. This book is my contribution to that memory.

CHAPTER 1

Happy Valley School was an outgrowth of the work of The Five Point House, a private charitable foundation organized in 1850 to relieve the distressed conditions of an area in New York City known as the "Five Point District." "How did they live in Five Points?" Gary F. Wills, one of America's best journalists, goes on to describe the conditions in an article: "Nastily, brutishly and often briefly."

When, after the 1832 Cholera epidemic, the mayor ordered the streets scraped of animal and human filth, a lady who had lived there all her life exclaimed, "I never knew the streets were covered with stones." In the 1849 epidemic, pigs rooting in the street were, a report said, "contaminated by the contact of the children." It was said that in death the victims continued the tenement system, buried six tiers deep.

Wills goes on to describe the conditions uncovered by "salvage archaeology" at a construction site in lower Manhattan. "Most Five Points buildings, the rubble from which is now fifteen to twenty feet below street level, contained a saloon. The police raided one in which forty-two customers were crammed into one small room, the corner of which on a pile of dirty straw lay a woman just delivered of a child. Famous gangs like the Plug Uglies, Dead Rabbits and The Roach Guard fueled the riots of 1863. They began as draft riots, became race riots, then turned to pillaging the rich. Regular Army units fought house to house to restore order. At least 2,000 New Yorkers were killed."

Another view of the terrible conditions that existed in the Five Points District was expressed in an article in the May 14, 1951 edition of *Newsweek*. The article was entitled "Five Points To Happiness" and is reprinted below.

"When, in 1850, the members of the Ladies Home Missionary Society of the Methodist Episcopal Church in New York discovered that the Rev. Lewis Morris Pease had not preached a sermon for two days, they severed their connection with him. His mission stood near 'Murderers' Alley,' in a Lower Manhattan area known as Five Points. This section was once described by Charles Dickens as an appalling 'world of vice and misery...men and women slink off to sleep, forcing dislodged rats to move away in quest of better lodgings.' Mr. Pease believed in a neighborhood with 270 saloons and several times that many dance halls and bawdy houses, preaching the Gospel was not enough. The following year he established the Five Points House of Industry, to educate and find work for the residents of the most dismal slum in America. Since then 43,000 children have been helped by the institution. In 1951 Frederick H. Allen, a tall, blue-eyed ex-Marine and also the President of Five Points House helped celebrate the 100th Anniversary of the institution by stressing the fact that youngsters helped by Five Points House are normal children whose parents can't care for them."

THE NEW MISSION HOUSE OF THE FIVE POINTS

The Five Points House of Industry owes its beginnings to the Ladies Home Mission of the Methodist Episcopal Church. For a number of years they had been determined to set up a Mission House squarely in the midst of the most extreme poverty and degradation the city could offer. They did this because they were touched by the misery and squalor in which families had to endure.

The plight and suffering of the children in that area spurred them into action. They were encouraged by the work of a Dr. Chalmers who had succeeded in setting up a mission in the slums of

London just a few years earlier. Rev. Luckey was appointed to purchase The Old Brewery for the Home Mission. Twelve years earlier it had been turned into a tenement for the homeless and those who could pay a few dollars a month. The living conditions were beyond belief and violence and drunkenness was a daily occurrence. After purchasing the building in 1850 it was torn down. The new Mission House was a five story building built of brick. It cost $36,000 to build. It had a chapel that could seat 500 people for the worship of God by the outcast redeemed from the streets. Over the chapel were twenty tenements consisting of three rooms each, in which poor and deserving families could live comfortable at the rate of five dollars a month. Beneath the chapel was a large school room for daily instruction.

The Five Points Mission was an immediate success. It became a focal point for the wretched community. It was a beacon of hope in a sea of despair.

Alcoholism was rampant in the area and the Five Points House would often aid those who wanted to reform their lives. It gave them a fresh start and a helping hand in getting their lives in order. In the first few years 1,500 people signed a Temperance Pledge to refrain from drinking alcohol. Children were enrolled in school and boys were taught trades that could earn them an income. Clean clothes were issued free of charge and medical problems were diagnosed. The women of the Mission Home kept records of individual cases and began to intimately know the problems of the people they served. Children were required to attend Sunday School and they clung to the moral precepts being taught.

The Ladies of the Mission published case histories in novella form and used the proceeds from these books to continue the work of the Five Points Home Mission. Local Business people made donations of goods and services to the Mission. The Pastor at Five Points Mission was often called out to serve the needs of the poor people for prayer vigils over a dying child or to pay the funeral cost of a destitute family.

Soon the work of The Five Points Mission attracted the Mayor of New York and he pledged $5,000. Plans were made to build a hospital and expand the services of the Mission. The experiment of building a Mission Home in the midst of great need proved a success and soon the work of the Five Points House of Industry would attract national and international acclaim.

CLAUDE BOORUM AND THE HAPPY VALLEY COLONY

The character and personality of Claude Boorum defined forever the kind of children's home Happy Valley was to become. Claude Boorum, a school principal in Garrison, New York, and a close friend of William Church Osborn was asked to become the first Superintendent of Happy Valley Colony in Pomona, New York.

Because of an epidemic of diphtheria in New York City, William Church Osborn and his wife gave 311 acres to the Five Points House of Industry so that the children housed at 442 West 23 Street in New York City could be exposed to a more wholesome environment.

Claude Boorum had been asked once before by Mr. Osborne to set up a school in Garrison, New York. He directed its operation for eight years when Mr. Osborne and the Board of Trustees of the Five Points House asked him to start up a children's home in Pomona, New York. Before attending Geneseo State College to become a teacher, Mr. Boorum had been a farmer. It was his love of farming and children and his boundless energy that guided the establishment of Happy Valley Colony for twenty years. When he left in 1930, over 155 children were residents in Happy Valley and another 280 children were in boarding homes. Mr. Boorum was directly responsible for the Boarding home program also.

The Farm House at Pomona became the first residence for boys at Happy Valley. Mr. Boorum presided over a building program that saw a water system installed and the erection of Eggleston College and the Jesup Memorial Administration Building and Chapel. Jesup Memorial was a gift of J. P. Morgan.

An electric lighting system was installed and the farm was expanded through gifts of Jersey cows, pigs, and farm equipment. Frederic E. Camp Cottage was built and occupied, then Wheelock and James Cottage were built to house the girls. Water towers were built to increase water pressure, then Ford and Camp Jr. Cottages were built and dedicated. In 1925 Mrs. Alexander Webb donated money to build the William Hamilton Russell Memorial Gymnasium. Perkins and Perkins Jr. Cottages were completed and occupied in 1928. In 1929 Weekes Cottage was built on a tract of land given to the institution by Frederic Delano Weekes. Edwin Gould donated the facilities for a summer camp.

Mr. Boorum commuted back and forth from Pomona to the Reception House at 454 West 23rd Street. Running the Boarding Home Program and Happy Valley Colony took great organizational skills and dedication. Mr. Boorum's presence was sorely missed when he resigned in 1930. He had taken 286 barren acres and created a home for hundreds of boys and girls who had previously known squalor and neglect. His long tenure as superintendent and his practical knowledge of farming and manual labor left a solid legacy of guidelines for operating the child care agency known as Happy Valley Colony later to be renamed Happy Valley School.

Bill Boorum, the son of Claude Boorum and his wife, was actually born on the grounds of Happy Valley. He shared many memories with me about those early years before the establishment of the cottages and an electrical system. He told me they would store milk in a spring in order to keep it cool and they unloaded coal from a railroad car. Oil lamps were used in the early years to light up the homes. He related fond memories of riding horses with some of the kids at Happy Valley and how his mother would become embarrassed at the number of kids who would follow his father as he toured the grounds.

Claude Boorum also began the practice of issuing monthly bulletins illustrated with pictures he took of the children and their various activities. He would give these bulletins to the Board of Trustees so they would have a more intimate feeling for the children under their care. Bill Boorum was kind enough to let me illustrate some of these pictures taken by Claude Boorum in my book. They give a picture of how it was to grow up as a child in the 1920's at Happy Valley Colony.

EDWIN GOULD: A FRIEND OF HAPPY VALLEY AND A TITAN OF PHILANTHROPY TO CHILDREN

Edwin Gould, son of Jay Gould, a notorious railroad magnate, was born on February 25, 1866 in a mansion in New York City. The second of six Gould children enjoyed great wealth. His father, a titan of Wall Street, was a loving parent who enjoyed his family. The boy enjoyed long, happy summers at estates on Long Island and Tarrytown, New York. He swam in the river, sailed near Tappan Zee and canoed for hours on the Hudson River. This love of nature was to remain with him all his life.

Edwin attended Columbia University. He was not an outstanding scholar but he enjoyed rowing and was on the Columbia University crew team. His father's annoyance at his failure to complete college led Edwin to set himself up as an independent broker and speculator. In less than a year he earned a million dollars and established himself as a reputable investor. His father's confidence in him was re-established and he was invited to join the family firm. When his father died, Edwin's fortune was estimated at twenty million dollars, eight of which he had made himself since leaving Columbia University.

He had always been a generous man but a specific incident would change his life forever. The unexpected death of his son Edwin Jr. at twenty-three, in a hunting accident in 1917, caused Edwin Gould to dedicate the remaining fifteen years of his life to disadvantaged, homeless children. His dedication to enhance the quality of life of children by the thousands both in America and abroad was to give him great peace of mind and much happiness for the remaining years of his life.

The scope of his philanthropic activities is simply amazing. His enjoyment of nature and the happiness of children caused him to set up summer camps throughout the United States. It is estimated that he personally paid for up to a million camper days for children. At Happy Valley Colony he built and donated two camp buildings and established a large camping program for hundreds of disadvantaged children. He continually made generous donations of time and energy to Happy Valley throughout his lifetime. In 1931 he took over the Boarding Home program from the Trustees of The Five Points House of Industry so that the trustees could devote their financial resources to the Pomona residence. The stock market crash of 1929 had severely depleted resources available to Happy Valley.

The Edwin Gould Foundation for Children was set up by special act of the New York State Legislature to centralize his many philanthropic activities. When he died in 1933 over ninety charitable institutions were beneficiaries of his will.

He is especially remembered for starting up Lakeside School, formerly The Messiah Home For Children in Spring Valley, New York. Lakeside School is still in full operation under the name of the Edwin Gould Academy due to Mr. Gould's foresight in establishing a foundation that gave broad scope to its trustees to act in any manner that benefited the welfare of children in New York State and in the U.S. The funds from the Edwin Gould Foundation continue to support the works of the Edwin Gould Academy and many other endeavors.

Not to be forgotten was his early commitment to the care of disadvantaged black children in New York City. He established the Booker T. Washington Home School on Boston Road in the Bronx and paid for all it operation out of his own expense. Eventually it was merged into The Edwin Gould Foundation for Children and his commitment to cultural diversity continues to this day. Mr. Gould is also remembered for his concerns for quality medical care for children and the establishment of scholarships for disadvantaged children.

Happy Valley Colony During the 1920's

The first cottage to be used for children, The Farmhouse, 1911

Claude B. Boorom
1st superintendent of Happy Valley Colony, he was superintendent from 1911 to 1930.

Happy Valley Colony During the 1920's

Children at the pond and mill that powered the first electrical system at Happy Valley.

Two boys going fishing.

Happy Valley Colony During the 1920's

Children waiting for placement at 23rd Street in New York City.

Learning how to be a mechanic.

Happy Valley Colony During the 1920's

Truck purchase to be used for hauling coal.
Children enjoy first ride.

Apple blossom time at Happy Valley Colony.

Happy Valley Colony During the 1920's

Commencement exercises bring members of the Board of Trustees to Happy Valley. Shown are: Mrs. Alexander Webb, T. Tileston Wells, President of the Board of Trustees, Mr. Edwin Gould, Wallace Reid, and his son (the chaplain).

Marshal Fields donates $2,500 for the purpose of maintaining Wheelock Cottage for girls.

Happy Valley Colony During the 1920's

Boys take part in doing farm work, dairying and poultry raising.

Boys build a raft and go for a sail on the pond at Happy Valley.

Happy Valley Colony During the 1920's

David Egleston Cottage dedicated in 1912.

Three brothers in foster care.

Happy Valley Colony During the 1920's

A family from Greece reunited at Happy Valley.

School days at Happy Valley.

Happy Valley Colony During the 1920's

F. Delano Weekes visits Weekes Cottage.

Halloween at Happy Valley.

Happy Valley Colony During the 1920's

Four boys from a Russian family arrive at Happy Valley.

A Japanese boy climbs a beanstalk at Happy Valley.

Happy Valley Colony During the 1920's

Edwin Gould, a welcomed visitor and generous trustee.

Afro. American children at a boarding house.

Happy Valley Colony During the 1920's

Fun in the snow at Happy Valley.

Working on the farm.

HISTORY AND PURPOSE

Happy Valley was a country home school for boys and girls in the first through the eighth grades, from six to eighteen years of age. It was dedicated to the service of children whose homes had been broken or who would benefit from school experience in homelike surroundings. If a child wished to remain at Happy Valley after completion of the eighth grade, he continued his education at the Senior High School in nearby Spring Valley.

The school is the outgrowth of the work of The Five Points House of Industry, a private charitable foundation organized in 1850 to relieve the distressed conditions of the slum area in New York City known as "The Five Points District." At its inception, The Five Points House offered those in need practical help in the form of food and clothing, and encouragement toward self-reliance by providing opportunities for work for children. The care of children soon became one of the most important areas of its work.

In all its work The Five Points House maintained a high degree of respect for the rights of the individual.

The children were offered the benefits of a homelike atmosphere, country living and good food.

The children often grew their own vegetables, milked cows and collected eggs from the chicken house under the guidance of the local farmer.

All meals were cooked and served by cottage parents.

Vocational courses were offered at the school. Mr. Mills, the carpentry teacher and longtime resident of Happy Valley, taught hundreds of boys hands-on experience in construction and cabinet-making. My brother, Dave and my brother-in-law Ron Fiorelli were later to put this experience to good use. Dave became a well-known local home builder and Ron, an advertising executive, often showed me renovations he had done himself at his home in Suffern.

SPORTS AND RECREATION

A well-balanced sports program was provided by the Director of Athletics. During the 1950's and early 1960's that man was John Kearns. We learned so many sports and games from Coach Kearns. We learned how to win, how to take a loss, fight fair and be a good sport. We marked the seasons by the games we played. During the winter basketball was the leading sport, and both girls and boys competed with other schools in league play. In the early sixties Happy Valley was a basketball powerhouse. Jimmy Perna, John's assistant coach, shared in those victories.

In the spring, softball and baseball were the great favorites and everyone played. Track, volleyball and other activities were also enjoyed. In the summer, swimming and water sports lead the way while autumn brought football and soccer with the boys and archery and badminton for the girls. As a kid, my job was to take care of the gymnasium. John Kearns had a big influence on my life. After being discharged from the Air Force in 1963 I took advantage of the G.I. Bill and majored in physical education at L.I.U. I worked for St. Vincent's Home for Boys in Brooklyn and the Lexington School for the Deaf while attending college. In dealing with children as a YMCA Director I tried to share that same love of sports as a vehicle to help a child grow.

HEALTH

The limited enrollment of the School made it possible to operate each cottage not as an institution but as a private home in a community setting. An abundance of fresh food fruits, vegetables and milk were provided in a consistently well balanced diet under the direction of a dietitian.

Complete physical examinations were required upon arrival and were repeated semi-annually. Dental care was provided. Mental hygiene was available on a non-treatment basis by a school psychiatrist.

Boys' sports: late 1940's – early 1950's.

Girls' softball team: early 1950's.

Sports team: baseball: late 1940's.

Happy Valley Baseball Team: early 1950's – Coach Kearns.

Interior of a boys' cottage.

Basketball team: 1951–1952.

Varsity girls' basketball team: 1950–1951.

Varsity girls' basketball team: 1951–1952.

Boys' varsity basketball team: 1951–1952.

Boys' grade school basketball team: 1951–1952.

Boys' grade school basketball team: 1950–1951.

Boys' varsity basketball team: 1950–1951.

Boys' varsity basketball team: 1952–1953.

Basketball action.

Earning a varsity letter: recipient Ruth Rivera and Coach Kearns.

Boys' varsity basketball: 1953–1954

Happy Valley kids group picture.

Boys' varsity basketball: 1954–1955

Jimmy Ashcroft

Richie Carney

Mid-1950's Grasshopper Baseball Team.

Dancing the night away after a basketball game.

The Grasshopper League

Girls' basketball player

Gaynelle Sayles

Kathy Free

Peggy Sayles

The post basketball game dance.

Jimmy McElroy   Jose Torres

Dance after the basketball game.

The best part of a basketball game: the post-game dance.

Hi there!

Ron Fiorelli

Post-game refreshments.

There's that Grasshopper Team again.

Dave Riley

Henry Carney

Phil Sayles

Grasshopper League Baseball Team.

Pete Carney

David Sayles

"Here, have a drink."

Summer fun in the gym.

Mr. Malamo: swimming instructor.

Lillian Towle and friends.

Hissan Khoury and a scene stealer.

Katherine Wenz and friend.

Carol Wenz set for a dive.

Gaynelle Sayles

"Hi. Who are you?"

1960 boys' varsity basketball team (championship team?)

Edith Gripper

Rita Reilly

Boys' Basketball Championship Team.

March 1960: Girls' basketball team group pictures.

Happy Valley beauties: 1956.

November 1959: grade school football team group picture.

"Watch me throw this shot put."

"Naw, I think I'll eat it instead."

Mr. Hendriksen leading a class trip to the UN: 1956.

Grade school gym class group picture: 1956.

A trip to the United Nations: 1956.

Grade school football team picture: 1959.

Spring grade school trip to the United Nations: 1960.

THE AMERICAN FEMALE GUARDIAN SOCIETY AND THE HOME FOR THE FRIENDLESS

In 1834 a group of Christian women and clergy gathered in New York City to discuss the plight of homeless females who were forced to enter a life of prostitution and degradation due to their friendless condition in large cities. New York City, a mecca for strangers and travelers from rural America, was being inundated with people living in squalid conditions and reduced to a life of crime to support themselves. They were refugees of the exploding Industrial Revolution. Untimely deaths of parents, sickness and addiction to alcohol and drugs left thousands of orphaned children. The complete absence of social services and access to medical care that we know of today caused a huge influx of people to be cast into the streets because of non-payment of rent or death of a household figure. The situation screamed out for remedy.

This gathering of Christian women and clergy came to be known as The American Female Guardian Society and they published a bi-monthly periodical originally entitled *The Advocate for Moral Reform and Family Guardian* later to become *The Advocate and Family Guardian*. This extraordinary periodical was published for almost one hundred years and the work done by The American Female Society was truly extraordinary. For over a hundred years this organization took in the friendless and the homeless and found homes throughout America for children as young as one year old up to eighteen years old. They initially only accepted females but this changed to accepting boys after a few years of operation. They opened boarding schools and operated twelve Industrial Schools throughout the country, many in large cities where boys and girls could learn technical skills in order to earn a livelihood. Hundreds of thousands of young children were saved from a life of poverty and destitution by the extraordinary efforts of this society whose only income came from donations and the sale of *The Advocate*.

While researching the history of a home I grew up in I came across the work of The American Female Guardian Society. While perusing material dating back from 1834 to 1965 I was touched by the heart-rending cases of children who came to the Society's attention. We can never know how difficult it was to live in the early and latter part of the 19th century. A close-knit and loving family suddenly splintered by the death of the breadwinner. A loss of a job, addiction to alcohol, medical problems, imprisonment of a spouse and eviction from a tenement caused severe dislocation and nowhere to turn. The American Female Guardian Society was there when government safety nets were non-existent. Through *The Advocate* church groups across the heartland of America responded and took in these waifs, orphans and abandoned children. They settled in small communities throughout America, were in most cases adopted and turned out to be good citizens.

Letter after letter to the AFGS from these children scattered throughout America attest to the good work done by this organization and how grateful the children were for their intervention in hopeless situations. In 1965 The American Female Guardian society merged with Woodycrest Youth Services. In 1972 Happy Valley School in Pomona, New York, began merger talks with Woodycrest Youth Services in the Bronx. Another merger in 1977 made the school Greer Woodycrest Children's

Services. The new institution phased out the boarding school and became a home for the developmentally disabled.

INSTITUTION CHRONOLOGY

1850---The Ladies' Home Missionary Society of the Methodist Episcopal Church announced their intention of including the Five Points House in their missionary operation. Rev. L. M. Pease was commissioned by the Society to open the field of endeavors. Day school started, women given employment.

1851---Under the control of National Temperance Society for ten months.

1852---Came entirely under the control of Rev. L. M. Pease.

1853---Sixty four acres of land purchased in the town of East Chester for a Farm School.

1854---At the solicitation of Mr. Pease, a company of gentlemen associated themselves together and formed a corporation--The Five Points House of Industry.

1856---The first building completed, which cost, with the land, $36,000.

1857---First Monthly Record published. Mr. J. M. Talcott succeeds Mr. Pease as superintendent but remains only a few weeks. Mr. Pease again in charge.

1858---Financial panic of 1857 caused unusual distress at the Five Points. Attendants at school provided with mid-day meal. Mr. B. R. Barlow appointed superintendent.

1859---Cow Bay converted into a playground, buildings around it torn down.

1860---Many Italians added to population of Five Points. Abraham Lincoln attended the Sunday Service at the Five Points.

1861---Many boys, former inmates of The Five Points House of Industry, enlisted for the war.

1864---Two-story building, 45 feet front and 90 feet deep, erected on the site of old Cow Bay.

1866---Farm at East Chester sold to Lutherans for an Orphans' Home.

1867---Working Women's Home opened.

1869---Two-story building torn down and new five-story building erected.

1870---Chapel on ground floor of new building dedicated.

1872---Working Women's Home closed.

1874---Manual Training inaugurated--shoe-making, tailoring, carpentry, and cooking.

1886---Hospital Building, four stories 25'x65' completed.

1887---Free Dispensary opened. Day Nursery opened. Building and repairs cost $438,000.

1893---Two stories added to hospital.

1895---Part of the building pronounced unsafe, weak foundation---boys' and girls' school removed across the street.

1896---New eight-story building completed and occupied.

1901---Gold Medal awarded by Department of Education and Economy for school exhibit.

1908---Hospital building sold and two top floors of old building outfitted for hospital. New plumbing and other changes.

1909---Epidemic of Diphtheria. Question of removal to the country suggested. Children moved to the country. Boarding Department inaugurated for some of the children. Apartments rented to accommodate the remainder. Office and Recreation House opened at 442 West 23rd Street, New York City. Fifty-six acres of land purchased at Elmsford, where it is proposed to build a Children's Village.

1909---A joint committee from the Boards of Trustees from the Children's Aid Society and The Five Points House of Industry, appointed to consider the question of cooperation between the two societies and recommended that the organizations be united under the management of The Children's Aid Society, keeping the corporate organization, The Five Points House of Industry intact for the time being.

1911---Plans of consolidation with the Children's Aid Society abandoned. Arrangements made to continue the use of the Children's Aid Society's properties until permanent quarters for The Five Point House of Industry could be provided. Two hundred and eighty six acres of land at Pomona, Rockland County, N.Y., presented to the institution by Mr. and Mrs. William Church Osborn. Upon this it was finally decided to build the Children's Village. Plans for the Elmsford Farm dropped. Farm House at Pomona Farm enlarged and occupied by boys.

1912---Advanced to the First Class by the State Board of Charities. Egleston Cottage and the Superintendent's Cottage built and occupied. Water system installed.

1913---Jesup Memorial Building and Chapel, and Russell Cottage completed and occupied. Minor improvements, piggery and ice-house built, electric lighting system installed.

1915---Frederic E. Camp Cottage at Happy Valley Colony, Pomona, N.Y., built and occupied. Five-story house, at 454 West 23rd Street, purchased and furnished and occupied as City Headquarters and reception station. The removal of the office and reception house from 442 West 23rd Street, to its own building, 454 West 23rd Street, constituted the final re-establishment of The Five Points House of Industry in its own building in the City.

1916---Wheelock Cottage and James Cottage, both for girls, built and occupied. Twenty acres added to the Cottage Colony by gift from Mr. Frederic Delano Weeks, upon which the new cottages were built. New water tower built of sufficient capacity and pressure to supply whole Colony. Complete laundry machinery installed. Playground equipped.

1917---Hugh N. Camp, Jr., Memorial Cottage and John Howard Ford Memorial Cottage built. Ario Pardee Clark Memorial Infirmary built and dedicated. Pumping station and toolshed constructed. A complete set of farm implements added. Manual training equipment acquired for the school.

1925---William Hamilton Russell Memorial Gymnasium, gift of Mrs. Alexander S. Webb, begun. Cornerstone laid on June 20, 1925, by T. Tileston Wells, president.

1926---Fifty-six acres of land at Elmsford, New York, sold April 30, 1926. William Hamilton Russell Memorial Gymnasium completed; dedicated on May 11, 1926. The donor, Mrs. Alexander S. Webb, attended the dedication and was presented with the keys of the gymnasium by the children.

1927---The Edward H. Perkins, Jr., and Norton Perkins Memorial Cottage built. The cornerstone was laid, with appropriate ceremonies, on June 24, 1927.

1928---The Edward H. Perkins, Jr., and Norton Perkins Memorial Cottage completed and opened April 14.

1929---The Weekes Memorial Cottage built on the tract of land given to the institution by Mr. Frederic Delano Weekes in 1916. Summer Camp for fifty additional children of Happy Valley Colony, donated by Edwin Gould, was built and occupied during the summer. A department for the care of black children instituted and children are boarded with black families.

1930---Mr. Gerald Pugh appointed superintendent to succeed Mr. Claude B. Boorom, who resigned on February 15, 1930. The Weekes Memorial Cottage dedicated on June 24, 1930; opened in July. Extensive repairs to buildings and grounds begin. Street lights installed. School program reorganized and teaching staff expanded.

1935---Walter Hendrickson comes to the school, eventually becoming superintendent. He begins policy of taking all races at the school.

1972---Merger with Woodycrest Youth Services in the Bronx

1977---Another merger makes the school Greer Woodycrest Children's Services. The new institution phases out boarding school and becomes a home for the mentally retarded.

1990---Greer-Woodycrest turns the school over to the state citing financial problems. Crystal Run Inc. is appointed to take over and set up community group homes for the residents.

June 1992---Alumni organize first Happy Valley Reunion in thirty years.

Oct. 30, 1992---Buildings are vacated to make way for Minisceongo Golf Club.

Former classmates reunite: Rita Fiorelli, Dale Riley and Annette Swann doing *The Stroll*.

'HAPPY' ARE THE MEMORIES

ALUMNI OF POMONA'S HAPPY VALLEY SCHOOL REUNITE AS SCHOOL IS TORN DOWN.

The following copyrighted article "Happy Are the Memories" appeared in the January 20th, 1993 edition of *The Rockland Journal News*. It was written by Tim Henderson, a staff writer and it was reprinted with permission of *The Rockland Journal News*. Tim Henderson visited the school as it was being torn down and he attended a reunion party where he met with many alumni and recorded his impressions.

HAPPY ARE THE MEMORIES

Tom Riley was looking for the tree, but he couldn't find it. Bulldozers groaned and wheezed over the rise as the cottages of the old Happy Valley School crumbled into rubble.

He was on the path between the girls and boys section, a great place for a rendezvous 40 years ago when he grew up at Happy Valley School. Riley's sister, Rita, who arrived with him at Happy Valley School in 1950, fell in love with Ron Fiorelli there—now they're married, with two grown children, and live in Suffern.

"It was a place where you could meet your girl and have some privacy," recalled Bernard Swann, who lived at the school from 1958 to 1968.

Home Away From Home

The children at Happy Valley School, open from 1911 to 1977, were torn from their own families by fate, poverty, or the whims of the state. But they found new ties on the 300-acre farm, which was a private institution that took wards of the state and some children who simply had no place to go.

"Not everybody's happy about their experience with the school. Some of them think they got a raw deal there," said Haya Khoury, now a Manhattan attorney. "But the bond that was created between them is what's something special."

Khoury was instrumental in bringing Happy Valley alumni back together, with the first reunion in decades over the summer and another last weekend. Ironically, it came just as many buildings were being razed to make way for a golf course.

"It's not progress, it's a deterioration of progress," said Swann. "We don't need any more golf courses. We need more places like Happy Valley.

No Racism

The families at Happy Valley were artificial but the love was real, the alumni say.

"There was no black and white. These were my brothers and sisters," said Swann. "Only later, when they left the school as young adults did they learn how sharply divided the races are."

"I didn't know I was black until I went into the Navy," said George Hancock (1966-72) at 38 the youngest of the group at Saturday's reunion in Nyack. In the Navy he faced pressure to choose between his white scuba diving partners and his black teammates in basketball. "It was like I was supposed to be black and hate all white people, or... well, I can't be white," Hancock said. "At Happy Valley, it wasn't an issue. It didn't come up."

Integration was a cause for Walter Henricksen, the school's superintendent until 1977, recalled his widow, Miriam "Adre" Henricksen. "He was more or less instrumental in persuading them that's what they should do," Mrs. Henricksen said.

Khoury also remembers the shock of seeing racism for the first time when she left Happy Valley. "I didn't realize the way things were until I got out, but when I got out, it really slapped me in the face," she said. I'm glad we grew up without it, because when it is inbred it's really hard to eradicate."

Hardwork

Children were raised in groups of 10 at each cottage, by "house parents." They did the work of farm children, plowing and milking before and after school. "Milking cows was the worst," said Adam Sebalos (1947 to 1960), now of Jersey City, N.J. "You had to get up at 4 am. My arms got so sore from all that milking. And when I got to school nobody would sit next to me, I smelled so bad."

In a way, it was a welcome respite from city cares, for children from big families with big worries. Jim McElroy, now of Chesapeake, Va., came from a home with 12 children. "You could just be a kid," he said of his stay at Happy Valley from 1950 to 1962. "You were safe, you didn't have to worry about money or anything. Everything was taken care of. It was a nice place to be."

It was the wonders of nature that made the best memories for Tom Riley, now a Nanuet postman who's working on a history of the school. "We were just poor kids from the city, from broken families," Riley said. "But here we had 300 acres to play in. We could play in the woods, build forts and tree houses, we had our swimming holes."

Together Again

Many alumni had lost touch over the years, especially since the school became a home for the mentally retarded in the late 1970s, and the grounds were then sold for a golf course in 1991.

As the old buildings came down—some will be retained and renovated as gyms and clubhouses—there was a strong urge to bring back the family for a reunion. Hancock, coincidentally, helped with asbestos removal at the old Jesup Hall, soon to be a plush golf club and restaurant overlooking the fairway. Pete Carney, an elementary art teacher and Hillcrest firefighter, helped put out a debris fire last month at the old Happy Valley grounds.

Khoury hopes to keep the family in touch. "Come back in another 30 years. We'll have another reunion," she said.

Eddie Gripper speaks to the alumni.

John Kearns addresses the alumni.

Camp Jr. Cottage for Boys.

GEORGE COSMOS, A FORMER HAPPY VALLEY ALUMNI FILLS US IN ON THE 1930'S AND THE 1940'S

I would like to thank George Cosmos of Eugene, Oregon for filling us in on life at Happy Valley School during the 1930's and 1940's. I first learned of George Cosmos and his sister, Irene when a reporter, Don Bishoff of *The Oregon-Register-Guard* did a story on orphanages and Newt Gingrich's promotion of them in his Contract with America. Don Bishoff called me and asked me for some input. It seemed he was doing a story on George and his sister, Irene. George was kind enough to send a number of photographs depicting some of the boys and girls living in Happy Valley School at the time. He also gave me a list of names. If anyone knows where these people might be and wants to contact George, you can write or call him at:

George Cosmos
1838 High Street
Eugene, Oregon 97401
Telephone (503) 344-8169

Many Happy Valley boys and girls served their country in the armed forces upon leaving Happy Valley. During World War II, a number were killed or wounded.

Happy Valley Joy Spreaders.

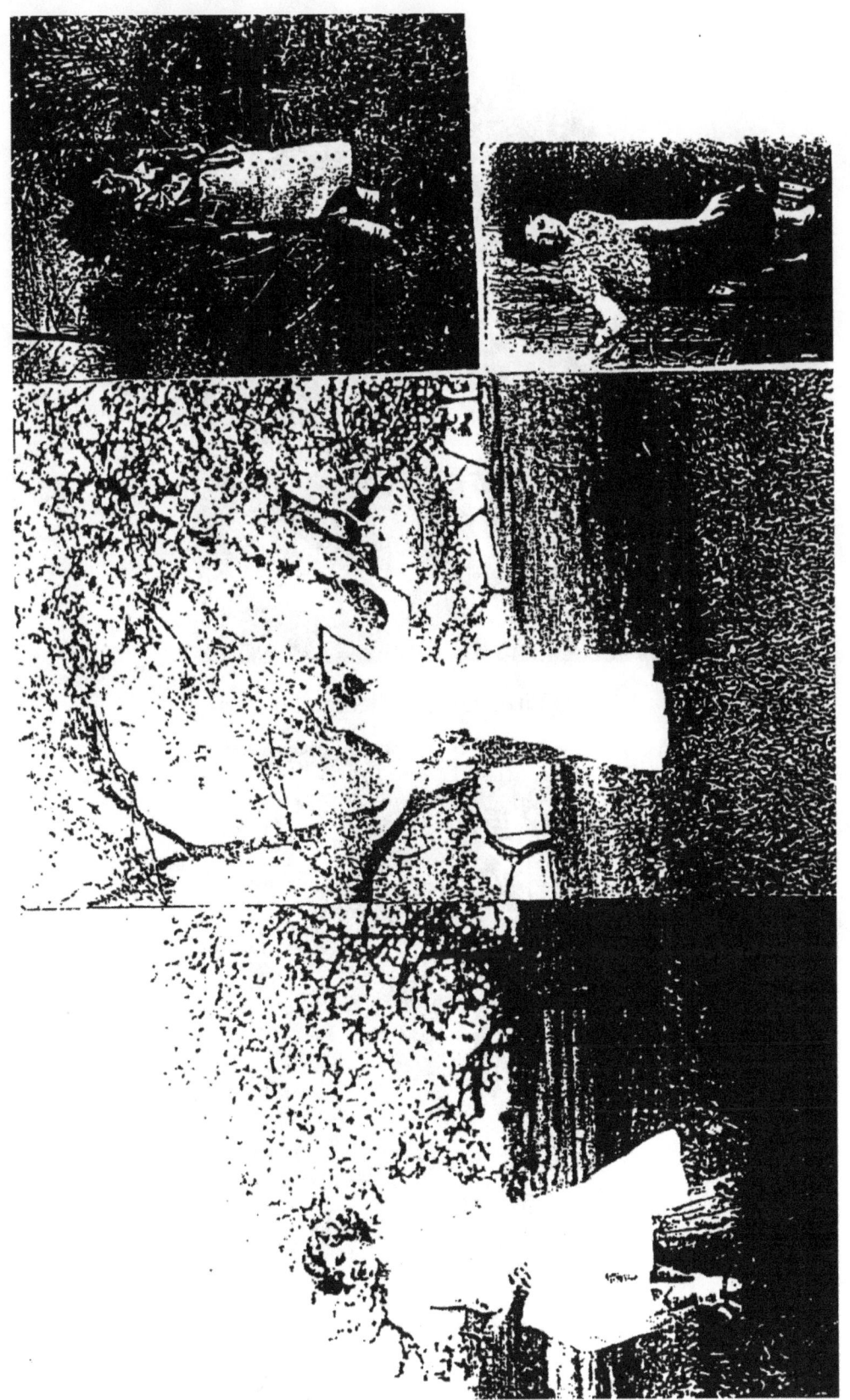

Peggy Monroe and Mia.

Victoria Fitzgerald and George Cosmos.

The Cosmos Family.

Boys eating watermelon in 1938.

Rosemarie and friends and family.

John Beckleman

Geo. Cosmos and Harold (Benny).

Plowing a field in 1938.

George Cosmos   Employees at Happy Valley School.

Mr. Frank Firth

George Cosmos

Pretending to fight.

Willie

Working on the chicken farm.

Plowing and farm work.

The Thinker.

Farm work.

First row (left): Rosemarie Shotack
Second row (middle): Irene Cosmos

Sitting under the apple tree.

Dress for the best outside the church.

A scene from 1939.

First row (left to right): Clinton Keith, Alex Dubin, Harry, and Basil Planakis.
Second row (left to right): Harold Schmidt, Henry Tasaka, Freddie Vicheller, and Walter Davis.
Third row (left to right): Willie Korokowsky, George Collyer, John Ladutleo, and Harry Keith.

1939

Sitting on the dock of the bay (1939).

Life at Happy Valley in the early 1940's.

There is a curious absence of material relating to the mid 1930's and 1940's concerning Happy Valley School. These were difficult years in our country, there was a worldwide depression and then a world war. Maybe it was because time and circumstances, such as earning a living, limited the time I could devote to research. For some strange reason I never could find the Annual Reports issued yearly by the Five Points House for this period in time.

    We do know William Henry Mandrey, Ph.D. was the director of The Five Points House and the Pomona residence. Dr. Mandrey was born in 1893 and he directed Happy Valley from 1935-1946. Dr. Mandrey had a long list of accomplishments. He graduated Amherst College and went on to receive a doctorate in philosophy from Yale University. He was a president of Arnold College in New Haven, Connecticut, and he served many years with the Connecticut State Department of Education before joining the Five Points House.

BOARD OF TRUSTEES

Albert R. Connelly .... President
Benjamin S. Clark .... Vice President
Clarence W. Bartow .... Vice President
Howard C. Adams .... Treasurer
Allen F. Maulsby .... Secretary
Montagnie Van Norden .... Asst. Treasurer
J. Ben Ali Haggin .... Asst. Secretary

Archie E. Albright	Henry Ives Cobb, Jr.
Clarence A. Barnes, Jr.	Hilary H. Holmes, M.D.
F. Gordon Brown	DeWitt Hornor

HONORARY TRUSTEES

Henry Cape, Jr.	John W. Hornor

OTHER CORPORATION AND COMMITTEE MEMBERS

Mrs. Howard C. Adams	Mrs. George Chase Lewis
Mrs. Lorenzo D. Armstrong	Mrs. Everett Mantine
George T. Ashforth	Mrs. H. von L. Meyer, Jr.
Mrs. J. Harper Bonnell	Richard W. Murrie
Mrs. Beveridge C. Dunlop	Miss Katherine P. Noble
Mrs. James N. Dunlop	Mrs. Ralph St. L. Peverley
Mrs. Lewis Epperson	Mrs. Calvin H. Plimpton
Mrs. Henry E. Gardiner	Mrs. Robert Pyzel
Mrs. Noyes Hamilton	Philip Rhinelander
James P. Hendrick	Mrs. Beverley R. Robinson
Mrs. Hilary H. Holmes	Mrs. Frank Russell
Mrs. John W. Hornor	Miss Joan Russell
Mrs. George H. Houston	Miss Jocelyn Sherwood
Mrs. Frederick B. Hufnagel	John C. Traphagen
Mrs. Harold Huntington Jacocks	Mrs. John C. Traphagen
Miss. Anna Kevelova	Mrs. Maurice P. van Buren
Mrs. Connor Lawrence	Miss Frances Williams

TRUSTEES OF THE FIVE POINTS HOUSE SINCE 1854

1854-1871	Archibald Russell	1876-1907	Charles Lanier	1923-1945	Francis L. Robbins, Jr.
1854-1882	Charles Ely	1879-1881	William W. Astor	1926-1934	John Wells
1854-1858	Thomas S. Eells	1879-1883)	Oliver Harriman	1927-1930	Edwin Gould
1854-1855	Henry R. Remsen	1885-1893)	Oliver Harriman	1929-1952	Andrew Chalmers Wilson
1854-1858	George Bird	1884-1900	Walter H. Lewis	1932-1947	Lorenzo D. Armstrong
1854-1856	Edward G. Bradbury	1885-1898	Henry E. Hawley	1932-1935	L. Gordon Hamersley
1854-1856	Charles B. Tatham	1895-1919	Archibald D. Russell	1932-1954	John W. Hornor
1854-1855	Wm. W. Cornell	1886-1904	Frederic E. Camp	1932-1942	Pierre Jay
1854-1855	George G. Waters	1898-1935	T. Tileston Wells	1935-1957	Henry Cape, Jr.
1855-1856	Horace B. Claflin	1901-1921	William H. Wheelock	1935-1946	James P. Hendrick
1857-1878	Frederick G. Foster	1903-1908	Charles F. Hoffman	1935-1948	Deering Howe
1855-1858	W. R. Vermilye	1904-1908	J. Hopkins Smith	1938-1951	Beverley R. Robinson
1856-1863	C. H. Shipman	1906-1908	Guy R. McLane	1939-1946	P. Erskine Wood
1856-1863	Hiram Barney	1908-1910	C. C. Cuyler	1943-1957	John Fiske
1855-1861	C. H. Dabney	1908-1920	Hugh N. Camp, Jr.	1946-1955	Albert B. Ashforth
1858-1874	Marshall Lefferts	1908-1915	Dr. Eugene H. Pool	1948-1957	Frederick H. Allen
1859-1885	Hugh N. Camp	1909-1914	William Church Osborn	1948-	Albert R. Connelly
1859-1860	Wm. Smith Brown	1909-1918	Evert Jansen Wendell	1948-	Benjamin S. Clark
1860-1862	John Slade	1909-1913	F. Delano Weekes	1950-	Henry Ives Cobb, Jr.
1862-1866)	R. B. Lockwood	1910-1911	Henry A. Murray	1950-	Dr. Hilary Holmes
1868-1869)	R. B. Lockwood	1911-1913	Edwin G. Merrill	1951	Clarence W. Bartow
1862-1867	Wm. T. Booth	1914-1926	A. Leo Everett	1952-	Howard C. Adams
1864-1884	D. Lydig Suydam	1914-1956	Harold Benjamin Clark	1953-	F. Gordon Brown
1864-1865	Josiah S. Leveritt	1915-1921	Norton Perkins	1957-1964	Richard W. Murrie
1866-1897	George F. Betts	1916-1918	Wm. T. Emmet	1957-1963	John D. Calhoun
1865-1866	Theodore B. Bronson	1919-1920	Dr. E. Fahnestock	1957-	Montagnie Van Norden
1868-1907	Morris K. Jesup	1919-1927	Frederic O. Spedden	1959-	Archie E. Albright
1871-1875)	George M. Morgan	1920-1951	A. Perry Osborn	1959-	Clarence A. Barnes, Jr.
1883-1905)	George M. Morgan	1920-1932	Wallace Reid	1963-	Allen F. Maulsby
1872-1878	A. Van Rensselaer	1921-1946	Howard Bayne	1963-	J. Ben Ali Haggin
1875-1907	David S. Egleston	1922-1932	Marshall Field	1967-	DeWitt Hornor

SCHOOL LIFE

The school day is preceded each morning by assembly in the chapel, with each child taking an active part in the non-sectarian service and in the current events discussion which follows.

School hours are from 9 to 12 in the morning and from 1:15 to 3:15 in the afternoon with an hour and fifteen minutes provided for a home-cooked lunch for each child at his cottage.

The subjects pursued during these hours comprise the basic ones required of an elementary school for accreditation in New York State. We have found that a child responds well and makes rapid progress in our small classes which are limited to ten or twelve pupils. Classrooms are light, airy and spacious.

The program has been further enriched by private instruction in Speech and Remedial Reading where needed, made available to children by our local school district under a plan sponsored by the United States Office of Education. Physical Education, Music Appreciation and Art are part of the regular school program, which also includes Shop for the older boys and Home Economics for the older girls. Piano lessons at a reasonable cost can be arranged for students who show talent and interest.

Jesup Chapel is the center of the school's religious life.

School's choir.

RELIGIOUS LIFE

Religious services are held every Sunday morning in the beautiful chapel at Happy Valley. The choir is under the direction of an experienced organist and many of the children enjoy participating in this activity. The services are non-sectarian Protestant. Children whose parents request other specific religious training for them are enabled to attend services of their choice in Spring Valley. Children are encouraged to say grace before meals and their prayers at bedtime.

The August Heckscher Foundation All-Purpose Athletic Field provides plenty of room for action.

Trees are for climbing.

Summer cook-out.

Seeing who can get the best tan.

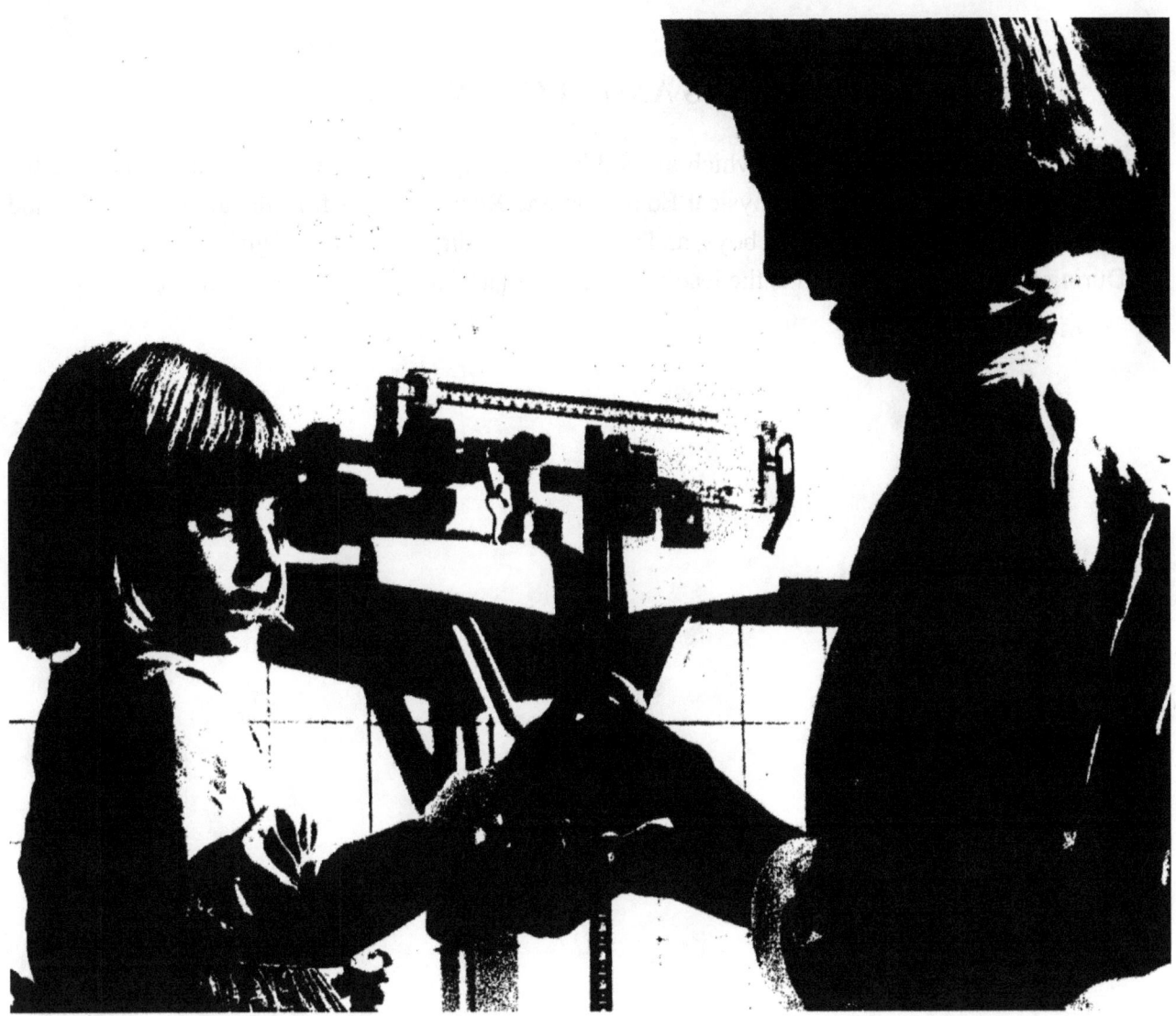

A nurse in residence and an on-call pediatrician provide good health care for the children at all times.

HEALTH

A carefully balanced program provides regular habits of work, play and hours of sleep necessary for continued good health. The school is noted for its good and abundant food provided in a consistently well-balanced diet.

The health of students is under the supervision of the school pediatrician and a resident nurse. Complete physical examinations are required upon arrival and are repeated semi-annually. Clinical care and special health services, where indicated, are provided by local hospitals or by Presbyterian Hospital in New York City. Semi-annual dental examinations and routine dental care are provided by the school dentist.

Mental health on a supportive, non-treatment basis is under the direction of the school psychiatrist, in conjunction with the social service staff.

SPORTS AND RECREATION

A well-balanced sports program in which all children participate is provided for each season of the year under the supervision of the Physical Education and Recreation staff. In the autumn, soccer and touch football are favorites with the boys, and archery and badminton with the girls.

During the winter, basketball is the leading sport, and girls' and boys' teams compete.

Dedicated teachers make learning interesting.

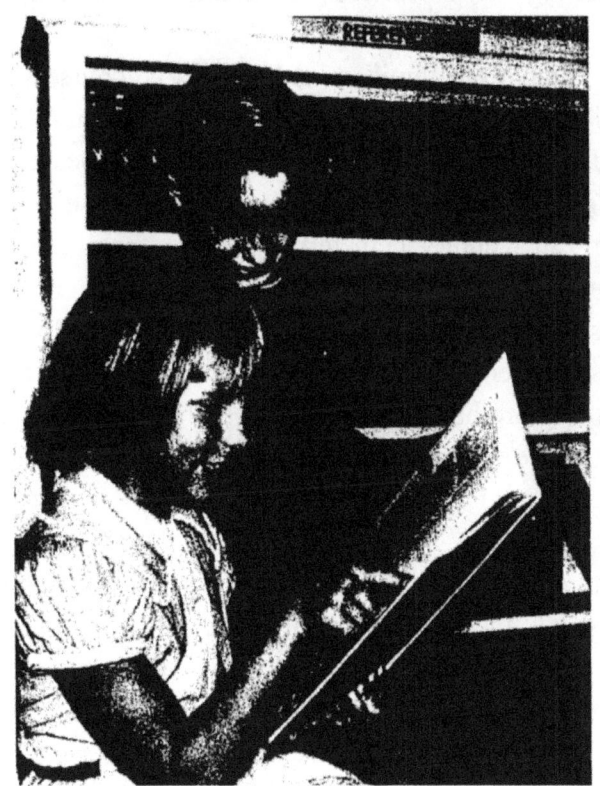

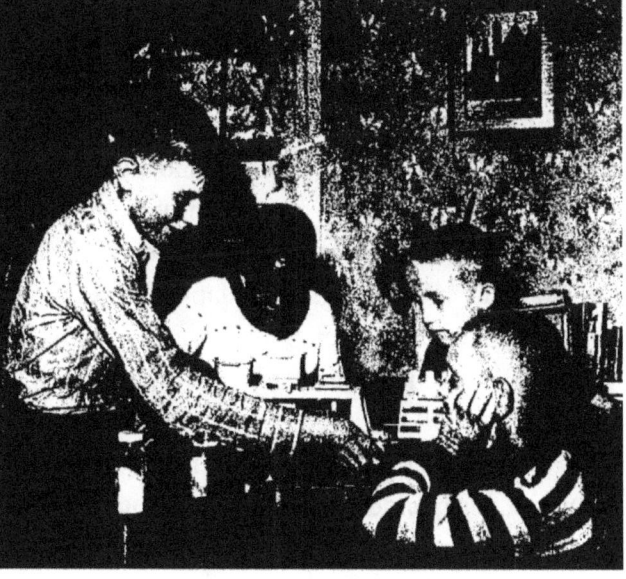

Time for fun, when homework is done.

Knowledge often is knowing where to go for information.

THE MINISCEONGO GOLF CLUB
FRIENDS PLAY GOLF ON THE SITE OF A FORMER CHILDREN'S HOME

The Minisceongo Golf Club, located at 110 Pomona Road in Pomona, N.Y., will soon become Rockland's premier golf club. The club had its grand opening in June of 1994. It's a dream come true for Eric Bergstol, a Rockland developer and avid golfer who saw the need for a new golfing facility that would harmonize the beauty of nature with the joy of golf. When Dave Redmond, a PGA Pro and manager of the Misceongo Golf Club, invited this reporter and several friends who had grown up on the very grounds where the club now stands to play a round of golf, we readily accepted the offer.

The Minisceongo Golf Club takes its name from a creek that runs through the course. The 160 acre property was purchased from Greer Woodycrest, a child care facility. From 1911 to 1973 the property had been called Happy Valley School, a home for neglected and dependent children. As I stood at the 1st tee with my brother, Dave Riley, my brother-in-law, Ron Fiorelli and my friend Jimmy Ashcroft I treasured the moment. Here we were forty years later, still relatively healthy and together playing a round of golf on the very grounds we had played all sorts of games as kids.

During my stay at Happy Valley School from 1950 to 1959 we had 311 acres to roam in; wildlife, nature and domesticated animals all about us. We built tree houses, underground forts, and made our own bow and arrows. We hunted snapping turtles in the wetlands and caught frogs and salamanders in the creek. We overturned old boards and rocks looking for snakes. We grew some of our own food and had fresh milk daily from cows kids milked.

Standing there with Dave, Ron and Jimmy we pointed out familiar landmarks. The course was designed by Roy Case, a renowned golf course designer who lets the terrain dictate the layout of the hole. All the positive qualities are retained and old growth trees are enhanced by beautiful landscaping. Minisceogo Golf Club will attract the golfing purist and nature lover. The course is not easy but it is so beautiful. Two large cisterns, an 18th century cemetery and lots of old growth hardwoods and a bridge over wetlands highlight some of the holes.

Dave and Ron were consistently belting drives. Jim is a physical education teacher at Spring Valley High School. He is also a former world class runner. The love of athletics imbued character into so many boys and girls at Happy Valley School. My brother Dave is a home builder and Ron has his own advertising agency. Midway through the 6th hole we came to a large walnut tree. Inscribed on the bark along with dozens of other inscriptions was a large *D* and the year *1954*. Forty years earlier Dave had inscribed it with a penknife.

As we played on, the excellent condition of the greens was pointed out. Robert DePalma, the former superintendent of Dellwood Country Club is now the superintendent of the Misceongo Golf Club. The clubhouse is still under renovation but it will soon be ready for full operation. During construction of the course, pottery, arrowheads and stone tools were unearthed. The find was catalogued and is now being prepared at Columbia University. It will be on display to members at the Clubhouse when it is ready. Thus far the find is dated to be from around the 7,000 B.C. era. As kids we knew first hand that the Indians had roamed this land. We constantly found arrowheads while picking carrots in the plowed fields.

Each hole is unique. The 3rd is especially challenging. A bridge runs over a large stretch of wetlands. A mighty drive is required from the longest tee. Choose the shorter tee the first time out. We learned from experience. The course played from the longest tee runs for over 7,000 yards. Happily there are four other tee lengths to choose from. The short course runs 4,920 yards. Over eight miles of piping feed the irrigation system.

The service rendered by the staff at Misceongo was impeccable. The staff is courteous and informative. A few tennis courts, a swimming pool, a restaurant and dining room will be available for members to use in the future. The pro shop is already in use and many golfing items can be purchased at a reasonable cost. There are presently 211 members, at last count. Dave Redmond is the PGA Pro and manager of the Minisceongo Golf Club. Tom Laszewski is his assistant. Amelia S. Wilk is the membership director. You can call (914) 362-8200 for membership information.

Dave, Ron, Jimmy and I had the feeling that Happy Valley was more of a place in and of the heart. The topography may change but the opportunity to play a round of golf with old friends was to be savored. Now many people can appreciate the beauty of nature and the joy of golf at a place called the Minisceongo Golf Club. It can only get better with time.

Dave Riley, a home builder, points to a tree on which he had carved his initials in 1954 when he was a child at Happy Valley School.

Graduating class from Photo School at Lowery Air Force Base in Colorado (1960).
The author is in the center of the front row.

DATA RETRIEVAL INVESTIGATIONS OF A MULTI-COMPONENT SITE AT THE MINISCEONGO GOLF COURSE, RAMAPO, NEW YORK

INTRODUCTION

The Minisceongo Golf Course site (known as MPS1) is a small multi-component station located in the Town of Ramapo, Rockland County, New York. MPS1 is located on a hilltop approximately 500-1000 feet south of the Mt. Ivy Swamp. MPS1 covers a total area of approximately 1.4 acres, of which approximately 0.93 acres will be impacted by construction of the proposed Minisceongo Golf Course. Construction in the area of MPS1 will consist of landscape modification, including cutting and filling of various areas to create fairways, greens and tee areas. A small area in the southeastern corner of the site will be cut away, while a large portion in the center of the site will be buried under several feet of fill. Impacts to the remainder of the site will be limited to the removal of small trees and brush. The developer has agreed to have these trees hand-cut rather than using heavy machinery, thereby avoiding impact to these areas.

In order to mitigate impacts to cultural resources in the area to be disturbed the project developer, Bergstol Enterprises, of New City, contracted with Hartgen Archeological Associates, Inc. of Troy, New York, to conduct data retrieval investigations of a portion of the prehistoric site. This document will present the research orientation, methods used and results obtained during the investigation of MPS1. Only the portion of the site that was proposed for development as of January 1993 was examined during the investigation reported herein.

Cultural material retrieved during these investigations indicate that the site was used throughout the Archaic stage of prehistoric cultural development. Temporally diagnostic artifacts recovered encompass the period from the Middle Archaic at approximately 5000 B.C. (Neville type projectile points) through the Transitional (Ritchie 1969) or Terminal Archaic (Snow 1980) Stage at approximately 1000 B.C. (Orient Fishtail type projectile points). The range of lithic material employed by inhabitants of MPS1 includes chert that outcrops in the Hudson Valley and other portions of New York, as well as argillite, shales, and jasper from Pennsylvania. The geographically dispersed lithic sources utilized suggest that MPS1 is located at a major crossroads of prehistoric travel and occupation. This is also indicated by the geographic position of MPS1, located in a gap between the Palisade Ridge and the Ramapo Mountains, near the headwaters of streams that run eastward to the Hudson drainage, westward to the Mahwah and eventually the Passaic drainage and southward to the Hackensack drainage. These drainages form part of a much wider network of prehistoric travel routes that connected central New Jersey with all of eastern New York, western Massachusetts and Connecticut, and southern Vermont.

During the late prehistoric period this area was occupied by an Algonquian speaking group known as the Munsee, or more generally as the Lenape. The Lenape had cultural ties over a wide area extending through southeastern New York, Massachusetts, Connecticut, New Jersey and the Delaware Valley of Pennsylvania. Culture ties of a lesser extent also existed with groups ranging from central New England south to the Chesapeake Bay.

Hartgen Archeological Associates, Inc.   March 1994

HISTORY OF INVESTIGATIONS

During the summer of 1991, Bergstol Enterprises of New City, New York, was in the progress of developing a 140 acre parcel, located in the town of Ramapo, Rockland County, New York, into the Minisceongo Golf Course. As part of the permitting process for this project, Bergstol Enterprises contracted Hartgen Archeological Associates, Inc. (HAA) to conduct a Stage IA Literature Review of the project for cultural resources.

The review (HAA 1991a) identified geological and hydrographic features within and adjacent to the project that would have been very attractive to prehistoric populations. These features include well drained soils on the hills overlooking wetlands, several small streams and wetlands, the Minisceongo Creek, which is the major drainage within that part of Rockland County, and the Mount Ivy Swamp, an extensive wetland adjacent to the project which covers approximately 170 acres at the northern terminus of the Palisades Ridge. Additionally, a survey of the prehistoric site files of the New York State Museum identified three reported sites less than one-half mile from the project and a fourth site within one mile. Local informants indicated that during the early part of the twentieth century prehistoric cultural material had been found in a now defunct orchard located within the eastern portion of the project. Based on the morphological features of the site, the proximity of four reported sites, and the information from local informants, a recommendation was made that a Stage IB Field Reconnaissance of the project to be undertaken.

The firm of Collamer & Associates (CA) was contracted by Bergstol Enterprises to undertake the Stage IB study (Collamer & Associates 1992) during December 1991. CA investigated the property through a combination of surface inspection of plowed transects and hand excavation of 30-45 cm. diameter screened shovel tests. CA's research design called for the excavation of 810 shovel tests placed at fifty foot intervals within areas that were to be disturbed by construction of the golf course. However, due to perceived previous disturbances or standing water, only 601 units were actually investigated.

In addition, 11,190 linear feet of plowed transects were surface inspected. This investigation resulted in the discovery of three prehistoric loci identified as Minisceongo Prehistoric Sites 1-3 (MPS1-3). Of these, MPS3 was determined to be an isolated find in a disturbed area and not in need of further investigation. MPS1 and MPS2 were determined to be in need of further investigation to decide if they met the criteria to be eligible for nomination to the National Register of Historic Places. Therefore, Stage II investigation of these two areas was recommended.

Bergstol Enterprises contracted with HAA to perform the Stage II investigations of the two prehistoric sites in March 1992 (HAA 1992a). The Stage II investigations had five goals:

i) determine the sites' boundaries;

ii) determine the temporal/cultural affiliation of the sites (when were they occupied);

iii) determine if there is a possibility for subsurface features to have been present and survived;

iv) collect data that will allow the State Historic Preservation Office (SHPO) to make National Register eligibility determinations;

v) determine what types of data are present and what types of questions can be addressed through investigation of these sites. (HAA 1992a:3)

In order to meet these objectives at MPS1, a survey strategy was designed which included excavating approximately fifty screened shovel tests around the Stage IB tests that had produced prehistoric cultural material. Each test was 45-50 cm. in diameter and excavated to a sterile subsoil. All soil from each test was sifted through 0.25 inch hardware mesh, and all prehistoric cultural material encountered was collected and labeled accordingly. Any historical cultural material encountered was noted but only a sample of this material was actually collected. A series of these tests was excavated in order to create density maps of artifact distribution to determine the limits of cultural material. The distributional data were used to determine the location of four 1 x 2 meter test units which were employed to increase the sample size and search for the presence of subsurface features. The following passage summarizes the results of this investigation:

The site consists of a low density scatter of lithic debris (generally 24 artifacts per 40 cm. test unit) distributed evenly across the site. In several areas the density of material increases indicating more intensive occupation. Stage II investigations consisted of the excavation of sixty, 40 cm. diameter, screened shovel tests. Thirty-six of the tests produced prehistoric cultural material with a range of one to eleven artifacts. Subsequent to the completion of these tests four 1 x 2 meter units were excavated to increase the sample size and to determine if subsurface features might be present. The locations of the 1 x 2 meter units were selected based upon artifact densities determined by the forty cm. tests. Altogether, 577 prehistoric items were recovered during the Stage II investigations of MPS1. This material consisted of 440 pieces of lithic waste, twenty chipped stone tools, seven utilized flakes, four rough stone tools and 106 pieces of cracked rock. The chipped stone tools consisted of twelve bifaces in various stages of production or discard, one drill and seven diagnostic projectile point forms.

The diagnostic forms indicate that at least three temporally discrete components are represented at MPS1 ranging from Middle Archaic (7000 B.P.) to Transitional Archaic (3000 B.P.). The oldest of these items identified were a Neville style projectile point, and a Neville or transitional between Neville and Kanawha styles. Both of these projectile points date to the early Middle Archaic stage (approximately 7000 B.P.). The second time period is represented by an untyped side-notched point that is similar to the Sylvan side-notched in many respects. This point dates to the Late Archaic stage around 4000 B.P. The third period of occupation falls within the Transitional Archaic (approximately 3000 B.P.) and is well represented in the collection by two different types of Fishtail projectile points, one Orient Fishtail and one Dry Brook Fishtail, a Susquehanna style knife made of a yellow to brown Pennsylvania jasper, and an untyped narrow stemmed point that is similar to Rossville styles of the Terminal Archaic to Early Woodland stage.

A single subsurface feature was also encountered. This feature was a pit, triangular in outline and deep-basin shaped in profile. The feature fill consisted of an unstratified dark organic soil with charcoal. Throughout the site, plow scars are visible at the interface between the topsoil and subsoil indicating that a plow zone exists. Because of this, it is likely that the upper portion of this feature bas been truncated. Artifacts recovered from the feature included a biface, several flakes and a large amount of cracked rock. Charcoal from this feature has been radiocarbon dated to 1690 A.D. ±70 years, indicating either a Contact period or Early Historic component, although no diagnostic cultural material associated with either of these periods were found during the Stage II. (HAA 1992b)

As this passage illustrates, Stage II investigations at 1 MPS1 determined that it is a significant site. Diagnostic materials recovered indicate a multi-component station with a depth of occupation of perhaps 5000 years. A surprisingly large number of tools were recovered compared to the density of the lithic scatter. Temporally diagnostic tools recovered indicate a time range for occupation of perhaps 7000 B.P. to 3000 B.P. The location of one feature indicated that other subsurface features might be present. Overall MPS1 appeared to have the potential to add a great deal to our understanding of prehistoric peoples in southern New York State and was determined to meet the criteria to be eligible for nomination to the National Register of Historic places. As a result of this determination, any impacts to MPS1 caused by the construction of the golf course would require some form of mitigation.

A similar Stage II testing strategy was employed for MPS2. At this location the initial Stage II investigation consisted of re-examining the plowed transects now that they had been subjected to a thorough washing by rain and snow for three months. Following the walkover, a series of 50 cm. screened shovel tests was excavated near areas of the transects that initially produced cultural material. Finally, a single 1 x 1 meter unit was excavated.

Stage II investigations at MPS2 revealed that the site consisted of only a few very scattered objects, representing isolated incidents. As such, it was determined that MIPS2 did not meet the criteria to be eligible for nomination to the National Register, and no mitigation was deemed necessary.

Based on the results of the Stage II investigations the current Data Retrieval Investigations were begun. Excavations were conducted in January of 1993. The weather during this period ranged from beautiful sunny days with temperatures in the 60° F range to snowy days with temperatures in the 20° F range. During the early part of the investigations ground cover consisted of a thin leaf cover. By the end of the investigations several inches of snow covered the ground, but did not impede the investigations.

SITE DESCRIPTION AND SETTING

The Minisceongo Golf Course Site (MPS1) is a multi-component site, approximately 1.4 acres in size, located on a wooded hilltop at approximately 440 feet above mean sea level (Photo 1, Map 1). The hill is located near the southern edge of a major upland wetland (the Mt. Ivy Swamp) near the headwaters of the Minisceongo Creek in the Town of Ramapo. A small unnamed stream runs below the hilltop along the east side of the site and into the Mt. Ivy Swamp. The South Branch of the Minisceongo Creek drains this wetland and then runs in a generally northern direction for two miles where it joins with the main branch and then proceeds in a generally easterly direction for four-five miles to its confluence with the Hudson River at Haverstraw Bay. The Minisceongo is a fast running stream over much of its length and contains many cataracts, rapids and small water falls. The natural attributes of this stream have been harnessed throughout recorded history as a source of power for several types of mills, including the Gamer Print and Dye Works (an important 19th century industry in the town of Haverstraw), and for recreational activities.

The Mt. Ivy Swamp is situated at the lowest elevation on an extensive plateau that extends in all directions. MPSl is located on the slope that leads up from this low point. The plateau consists of a series of undulating hills ranging from 400 to 600 feet above sea level, with most averaging around 500 feet. Beyond this plateau to the east is a slow steady descent to the Hackensack River Valley some four miles distant from MPSl (it should be noted that the streams which form the headwaters of the Hackensack River come to within less than one mile of MPSl near the base of the Palisade Ridge). To the west the plateau continues to the Mahwah River Valley, located at the base of the Ramapo Mountains. To the north the plateau continues until it reaches the base of Cheesecote Mountain and its foothill of Camp Hill; and to South Mountain which forms the northern terminus of the Palisades Range. The Minisceongo Creek flows north on the plateau and follows a natural break in the hills between Cheesecote Mountain and South Mountain, forming a natural travel corridor that continues to the Hudson River.

MPS1 is located at the juncture of three prominent geological formations (Figure 1). The site sits near the northern terminus of the Palisades Ridge, a forty mile long formation that runs southward to Staten Island. The Palisades Ridge near MPSl consists of an igneous dike of fine grained diabase that protrudes through sedimentary rocks of the Triassic redbeds of the Newark Basin. The sedimentary rocks near the dike "have been metamorphosed by the heat of the intrusion, producing bard quartzites from original sandstones and fine-grained-unifoliated 'hornfels' from shales". (Van Diver 1985) The area of the site itself is underlain by fairly level redbeds (red sandstone and shale) of the Newark Basin, which continue on to the south for a great distance. This formation consists primarily of conglomerates and sandstones that formed during the Upper Triassic. Within two miles to the west of MPSl are the Ramapo Mountains, and one mile to the north is Cheesecote Mountain, which together make up part of the eastern boundary of the Hudson Highlands. The Highlands are composed of complexly deformed gneisses, quartzites and marbles that extend from Pennsylvania to Connecticut (Van Orden 1985:55-68).

Hartgen Archeological Associates, Inc.   March 1994

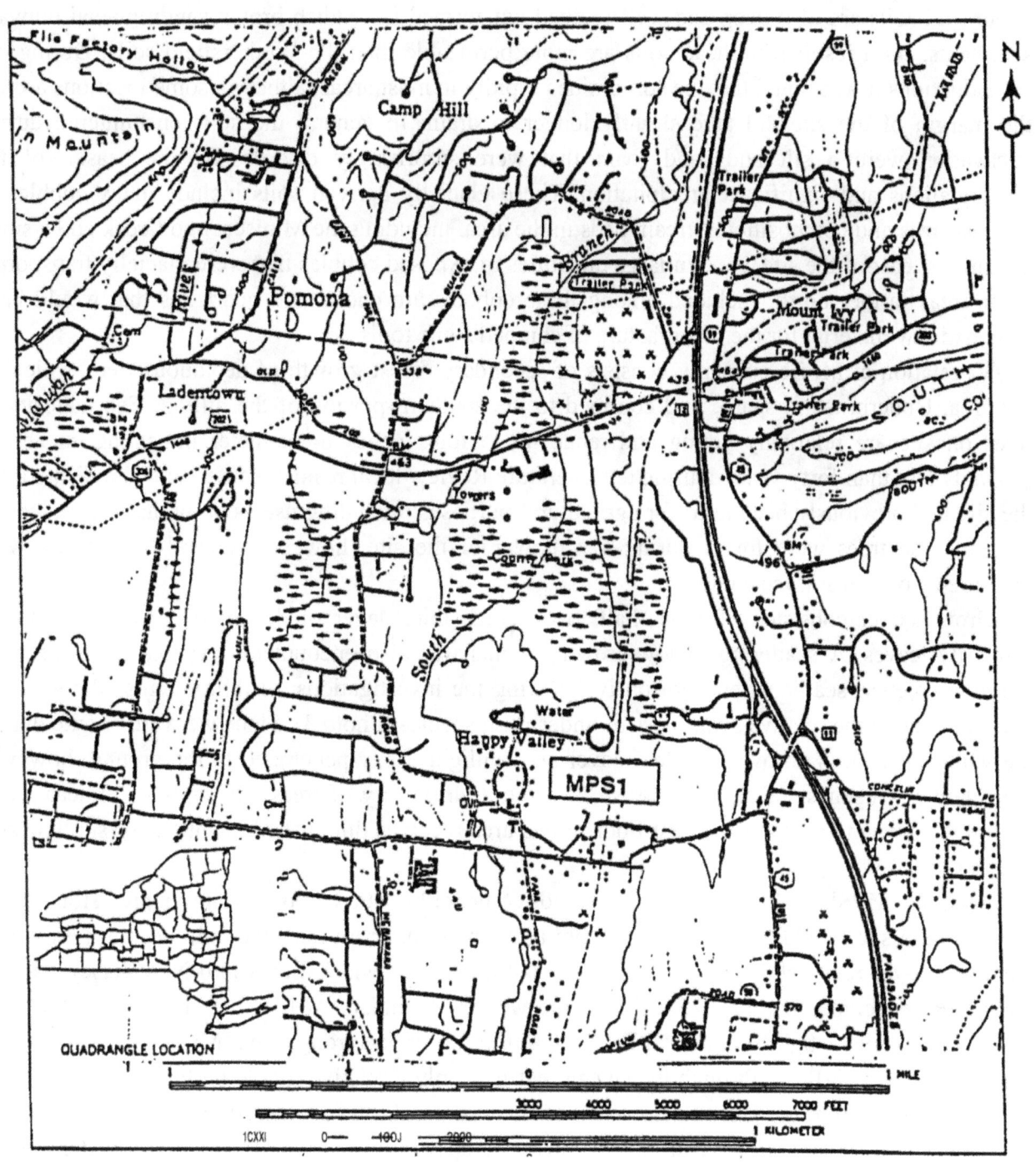

Map 1: Location of MPS1
NYSDOT Thiells 7.5' Quadrangle.

Soils at the site consist primarily of Wethersfield gravelly silt loam and Riverhead fine sandy loam. Wethersfield soils are deep and well drained, formed in reddish brown sandy glacial till, while Riverhead soils are also deep and well drained but formed in reddish brown sandy glacial outwash sediments. As a result Riverhead soils are more permeable than the Wethersfield soils. During our investigations it was noted that the soil drained rapidly in most areas, although some locations around the margin of the site did take slightly longer to drain. In general the soils encountered during excavation were a silt and sand loam that were surprisingly dry despite the season of the investigations and significant precipitation. These glacially derived soils include many cobbles of various sizes and composition. Stream beds in the area, including the Minisceongo Creek and a small stream just east of the site, contain large quantities of exposed cobbles that were glacially transported from areas farther north. Included among these cobbles are cherts and quartzites that would have provided raw material for the manufacture of chipped stone tools.

Vegetation at MPS1 currently consists of secondary forest growth of deciduous trees typical to the area. Underbrush is sparse and confined to the southern portion of the hilltop. The majority of trees on site are relatively young and range up to four inches in diameter indicating an age of probably less than forty years. During the Literature Review local residents interviewed indicated that the site had previously been used for agricultural purposes, including use as an orchard. No signs of orchard type trees were found during a walkover of the site, however, several cherry pits were identified from subsurface contexts.

Groundcover consisted of a one-half to one inch thick layer of decomposing organic matter, primarily leaves. A scattering of low-growing plants was also encountered. Typical of these were Virginia creeper, scallions, and poison ivy. During the investigations, visibility across the site was excellent due to the relative sparseness of underbrush species (Photo 3). Since we were on-site during the winter there was no overhead leaf cover and sunlight easily penetrated to the ground, however, the relative sparseness of the underbrush, and the high density of trees and saplings indicates that during the growing season the forest floor in this area receives diminished quantities of sunlight due to leaf cover.

Access to MPS1 is relatively easy since roads come within 500 feet of the site. In prehistoric times access to the site would have been easy from any direction. From the south and west access would have been over relatively flat, dry land. The Mahwah River, which flows into New Jersey and the Passaic River, comes within 2.25 miles of the western boundary of MPS1. Access from the north would have been slightly more difficult, requiring a trek through the Mt. Ivy Swamp. The Minisceongo Creek flows through the swamp but it is only a relative trickle on the south side of the wetland. Access from the Hackensack River to the east would have required an ascent of more than 500 feet over a distance of several miles. Travelling upstream (and uphill) to the headwaters of the Hackensack River would have brought travelers to within 4000-5000 feet of MPS1. In some areas this ascent has slopes of 50% or better, but these areas could be circumnavigated.

Hartgen Archeological Associates, Inc.					March 1994

Photo 3: View north across the site depicting the density of vegetation and typical groundcover. Note the relative lack of scrub species and the narrow diameter of the trees.   March 1994

STAGE III INVESTIGATIONS

INTRODUCTION

Potential impacts to MPS1 due to the construction of the golf course were to be limited to an approximately thirty-forty meter wide strip running in a generally northeast southwest direction through the central portion of the site. This area was to be totally cleared of vegetation, stripped of topsoil and landscaped to form a level tee area for the 6th hole of the golf course. Landscape modification included changes in elevation, including raising much of the area. Additional impacts to other portions of the site included removal of small trees and shrubs to allow more sunlight to the area and to "improve" the visual aspects of the course. The removal of these trees and shrubs was to be accomplished with hand tools.

In order to mitigate the impacts on the cultural deposits in the area to be disturbed, Bergstol Enterprises contracted with F.IAA to conduct resource recovery investigations on a sample of the site. The field investigation of MPS1 was conducted from January 4 to 22, 1993. Twenty-seven 2 by 2 meter units and three 1 by 1 meter units were examined (111 m2, 1,195 ft2). Nine features were identified in the field, several of which are prehistoric in nature. Diagnostic artifacts were recovered that date from the Middle Archaic (approximately 7000 B.P.) through the Transitional or Terminal Archaic Period (3500 B.P.) indicating a range of occupation of approximately 3500 years. A carbon sample retrieved from Feature 9 was subjected to C14 dating by the Beta Analytic Laboratory and returned an uncorrected date of 4570 ± 80 years B.P.[1] When corrected for fluctuations in atmospheric carbon (Ralph, Michael and Han 1974) the sample dates to 5420-5170 B.P. (3470-3220 B.C.)

RESEARCH POTENTIAL

In general, little is known about the archeology and prehistory of Rockland County. This can be attributed to several factors including the rapid, early industrial and residential development of the county, and a relative lack of professional or avocational investigation and publication in this region. Based on the data retrieved by the Stage IB and Stage II investigations, MPS1 was deemed to have the potential to provide data relevant to the following research questions. (HAA 1992b)

[1] Years B.P. are measured from 1950 A.D. to set a standard for comparison.

1) The upland location of the site suggests that it represents a hunting camp or some other specific resource utilization/acquisition location, when the multi-component nature of the site indicates that the available resources were important to temporally diverse cultures. Investigation of this site will provide data on diachronic usage of the resources and allow an examination of how resource utilization may have changed over a period of several millennia.

2) The presence of Middle Archaic material provides an opportunity to learn more about components of this rarely encountered stage in New York.

3) The site may contain a contact period component. Although historical documentation indicates that Rockland County was heavily populated by aboriginal people at the time of contact,

little archeological research concerning this period has been conducted in the region. Many of the major village sites of the native inhabitants, which were located along the Hudson River and other major waterways, have no doubt been disturbed or destroyed by industrial and residential development. MPS1 provides an opportunity to examine how people of this period may have utilized an upland environment and how that may have contributed to their survival in the face of European expansion and diseases.

4) The lithic material recovered from MPS1 came from of a wide variety of sources (various types of chert, quartz, and argillite, and jasper). This variety of material indicates that at least some of the inhabitants of MPS1 may have been involved in a regional trade network that extended westward into Pennsylvania, south into New Jersey and north into the interior of New York State. Further investigation will help to determine what temporal period, or periods, of occupation may have been involved in this network, and examine how trade relations may have changed over time.

5) Examination of the types of tools recovered and the edge-wear on these tools will help to determine the range of subsistence activities that were conducted at MPS1. Examination of the tools associated with different temporal periods will help to determine if use of the site varied over time.

    Hartgen Archeological Associates, Inc.   March 1994

Top photo: Eddie Gripper, Bernie Swann and Jimmy Ashcroft

Left to right: Ron, Jimmy, Pete, Rita and Mel.

Taken in 1926.

Alumni gathering.

Pete and Jim, responsible for getting the work done for alumni gatherings.

Alumni gathering.

1926 photo.

Painting by Pete.

Mel, Jim and Pete.

Mel making a documentary about Happy Valley School.

An alumni gathering.

A scene in one of the cottages.

A Happy Valley gathering.

Former athletic director John Kearns.

Coming out of church.

www.ingramcontent.com/pod-product-compliance
Lightning Source LLC
Chambersburg PA
CBHW080550170426
43195CB00016B/2747